THIRD PERSON

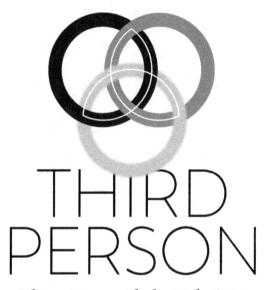

THIRD PERSON

Thirty Days with the Holy Spirit

AMY W. VOGEL

Seedbed

Printed in the United States of America

Cover design by Strange Last Name
Page design by PerfecType, Nashville, Tennessee

Vogel, Amy W.
Third person : thirty days with the Holy Spirit / Amy W. Vogel. – Frankin, Tennessee : Seedbed Publishing, ©2018.

pages ; cm.

ISBN 9781628245424 (paperback : alk. paper)
ISBN 9781628245431 (Mobi)
ISBN 9781628245448 (ePub)
ISBN 9781628245455 (uPDF) BS680.B8

1. Holy Spirit--Prayers and devotions. 2. Spiritual exercises.
3. Devotional calendars. I. Title.

BT121.3.V63 2018 231.3 2018940864

Seedbed

SEEDBED PUBLISHING
Franklin, Tennessee
seedbed.com

This book is dedicated to Jesus and my husband, David.
You are the two most important men in my life.

Contents

Acknowledgments

There are so many people who contribute to a book, even a small one like this. I wish I could name you all, but know that if you have crossed my path in life, you have made a contribution to this work.

I would like to thank the Seedbed team for trusting me, a complete unknown. You see the vision of what the Holy Spirit wants to do in the church in this day and age. You work tirelessly to see the church awaken to that vision and I bless all of you for responding to God in that work.

To Pastor Andy Cunningham—thank you for giving me the mission to write something about the Holy Spirit and the liberty to do it my way, as well as the connection point to the ones who are getting it out there.

To my pastor, brother, and friend, Christian—you have provided me the opportunity to dive into my gifting, only offering well-timed advice when I was about to go off the rails. Thanks for being my pastor as long as I need one.

This book would have never have happened without my girls: Johanne, Moseka, Wynter, Kim, Cindi, Janice,

Audrey, Jackie, Anita, Gindi, Gigi, Jessica, Sharon, Leslie, and Lynn. You are my sisters of heart. It is my honor and privilege to walk through this world, and into the next, with you. Thank you will never be enough.

To Mom—thank you for always knowing I would do something worthwhile and being proud of me for just being me. To my brother, Craig—you are always and forever my big brother. You have my love but, more importantly, my respect.

To my children: Natalie, Sophia, and Ella—you are God's greatest gifts to me in this world. Nothing will ever compare to seeing God form you into women who love Him and know what He is calling you to do. Thank you for your patience and encouragement, both in being your mom and letting me give so much of myself to others.

And, finally, to my husband, Dave—thank you for your unfailing protection, provision, and belief in me, no matter what. I am proud to be your wife.

Introduction

God in the third person is more than semantics. It is the reality of our life as Christians. It is also our privilege to live in communion with Him. It hadn't occurred to me that the Holy Spirit was a person wanting a relationship, just as much as the Father and the Son did. Then, I read Francis Chan's *Forgotten God*, and got involved in a women's study focused on the Holy Spirit. I read quite a few books on what is termed "the victorious life," or as Jesus referred to it in John 10:10, the abundant life here on earth He came to engage us in. The switchboard to the Holy Spirit really started to light up.

A great deal of my effort for the last fifteen years of believing in Christ (more than thirty if you count being saved at a DC Talk concert at age fourteen) has taught me many lessons. The biggest one, and a repeated theme, is that this life with Jesus was never meant to be a solitary expedition. It wasn't meant to be a trek that breaks you; it's meant to be an adventure in getting to know God. At times, that certainly has meant breaking and breakthrough. I've found the center of it: the Spirit of God is constantly teaching me how to be aligned with the mind and heart of my Father in heaven.

I haven't always known it was the Holy Spirit. It's only been recently when I've begun to look at the third member of the Trinity as someone who wants to be known. It's a challenging concept admitting I have God on the inside. Moving from that mind-blowing reality into a place where He wants to engage with me daily is quite a mystery I accept because it is what it says in the Word. I don't always get it. I have a friend who often reminds me I don't talk to the Lord "out there," but (as she points to my heart) "in there." Have you ever tried to talk to your chest? It's awkward.

To grow in my own faith, I needed to know more about this third person of the Trinity. I began this project from the beginning of Scripture to focus on the major themes of what and how the Holy Spirit thinks; how He is connected to the other two members of the Trinity; and how He has operated in the past so I can begin to grasp the idea of how He is operating in my present. These devotionals are a product of sitting with the verses, listening, and tying them into my personal history.

My eyes have been opened to these perilous times. We need the power of God the Holy Spirit brings. We need it personally to be conformed into the image of Christ and corporately to stand for the truth of Christ.

There is no other way we can overcome the cultural, political, and social calamity in our midst. We can't persevere without Him. We can't build Jesus-like character without Him. We can't be filled with hope without the Holy Spirit.

The good news is (and always has been) that His desire is to put Himself into our time and space. He is overjoyed when we ask Him to make our bodies temples of the living God that can make the kingdom of God available to all. He delights to enable and empower God's children to live like it. We need that now. We need Him now.

I hope these next thirty days are rejuvenating for your spiritual life. They have been for mine. To live from the place of access to God all the time is a marvelous feeling. It brings me peace and security I've never felt before. I've witnessed miracles I read about in the book of Acts. Scripture is indeed quick and powerful, sharpened by the presence of the living, breathing, and personal Spirit of God.

DAY 1

Creative Imagination

> The earth was without form and void, and darkness was over the face of the deep. And the Spirit of God was hovering over the face of the waters.
>
> —Genesis 1:2 ESV

How do you start to engage with the One who, as Eugene Peterson translates this verse in *The Message*, "brooded like a bird" over the waters? Let's start with the pronoun, *He*. The Holy Spirit is a He—a person—and a real living, breathing, relatable person. He has identity, feelings, and responses. He isn't necessarily in a *form* we understand. He isn't human like Jesus. He is the Spirit of Jesus, which means He is alive. The Holy Spirit is here; He is present, real, ready, and waiting.

In this passage, He is hovering and looking things over. He is waiting on His cue to be the agent of creation and change. He is anticipating and excited about what is to come. He is complete: the fullness of God, lacking nothing—even as He is surrounded by nothing. This person of God is God. He is the starting point, the Alpha and the Omega. He is the "bang" in the big bang, even before there was a perceivable bang. He created light and space. This was *kairos*—time before time was created, and where there is only eternity. This kairos begets something new—*chronos*, our time-based reality. The Holy Spirit is a mother who delivers the universe into being.

I like to try to picture what He looked like hovering there in patient, pregnant waiting. He is waiting for the perfect timing of God—the moment to speak and begin. Having been there when three children were born, I can imagine the atmosphere of intense anticipation. Perhaps the angels around the throne that sing, "Holy, Holy, Holy," held their breath in silence for a split second just before the Lord spoke.

These are fanciful imaginings; yet, I believe the Holy Spirit is worth dreaming about. He is worth getting to know and thinking about. To our church in this day and age, it is like seeking out a long-lost friend or relative. Francis Chan wrote a book about the Holy Spirit called

Forgotten God; and indeed, it seems He has been benched instead of given the opportunity to play in our lives.

In Peterson's translation of this verse, the Holy Spirit is waiting, like a mother bird waiting for the egg to hatch. He is still waiting for us—for our own desire to go deeper with God. Who better to engage with than the One whose job it is to reveal mysteries and explain all things; and the One who consoles, teaches, and even perfects our prayers so that they line up with God's will?

It is important to see in this imagery that He is over, not yet on or in. He is not yet a part of His creation—not yet joined with it. But in the creating, He is leaving a part of Himself. The Holy Spirit finally fully joined in the person of Christ and in the new church after Pentecost. Still, He has always been present. He wants to be joined with you and me. The Holy Spirit is still full of the excitement of the creation and of the possibility for each day. He is excited about the possibility of today. He hovers. He waits—for you. Will you reach out to meet Him?

Prayer

Come, Holy Spirit. I long for a deeper connection with You—the One who was present at the beginning and is present with me now. You are waiting on me to reach for You, and I am. Join with me today to better understand what it means to be in relationship with You and all the possibilities that holds. In Jesus' name, amen.

Thought

What God-possibility can the Holy Spirit birth in your life right now?

Group Discussion

1. Using your creative imagination, how do you envision the conversation in the Trinity prior to the act of creation?
2. How does the calling out of the Holy Spirit's presence change or challenge your perspective on the creation narrative in Genesis 1?
3. What situation in your life is formless and void that you want to see the Holy Spirit hovering over?

DAY 2

It's Not Just Me

The Spirit of God has made me, and the breath of the Almighty gives me life.

—Job 33:4

I have more than four decades of practice at thinking small. It has taken a work of the Holy Spirit to get me to look behind just what I see at my eye level. I've felt an active work—a persistent reminder—to stop leaning on my own understanding (see Proverbs 3:5). The Lord has been saying, "Okay, enough of thinking like you, Amy. Start practicing thinking like Me."

When I realize I'm applying my own understanding, instead of feeling guilty, it has become quite the relief. When I remember I'm not in charge or in control—not the one responsible to figure out absolutely every potential scenario and what-if—I nearly laugh out loud in joy.

There is immense freedom in being able to turn to the Holy Spirit and ask, "What do You think?" Like a fresh wind blowing in, I take a second and breathe deeply of His wisdom. I meditate on the impossibilities He can pull off, and focus my gaze on what He can do that I can't possibly achieve myself.

There are times I want to scream from the mountaintop, "I don't have to figure it out all by myself! Hallelujah!"

To actively turn to God with a feeling, circumstance, or relationship is one of those paradigm shifts of faith. When we do that humbly and expecting an answer (also called faith), I believe it makes the Lord very happy. What parent, pleased with his or her children, wouldn't respond with enthusiasm? Because it is God, He will also provide over and above what is needed—immeasurably more than we can ask or think (see Ephesians 3:20).

When you apply this renewal of your mind—to ask for the Holy Spirit's thoughts—it becomes the moment when the blinders come off. It is then you start to experience life with much more color, goodness, and wonder; and you will never want to put the blinders back on. When you give over to the truth that the almighty God has given you a life to live and is helping you to do it His way, it will wake you up to grab hold of bigger, better, and higher thoughts and ways.

I know this seems a very simple act in a world that values complicated thought. Still, when it is all you, you are all you have. When it is all God, you have infinite resources at your disposal. The more you turn to the Holy Spirit, the more you develop a secure, ridiculous, and joyful hope that everything is possible. I am close with some people whose very lives testify to this reality. My own life is marked by miracles. He has been there for me; He made me. Even when I thought I didn't have much to say about God, I see I wouldn't be here without His remarkable life-giving Spirit in me and keeping me close.

He is ready and willing—being the giver He is—to fill, refill, restore, and refresh. He is anxious to help, if I could use such a term. He wants to release His life into mine. It is that fresh wind of Himself that keeps me in line with His way. He raises my eyes to the hills to see "my help comes from the Lord, the Maker of heaven and earth" (Ps. 121:1–2).

Prayer

Come, Holy Spirit. Give me the life Jesus promised—full of abundance, and that is dependent on You and not myself. Help me to practice engaging with You in every situation and trusting Your insight and resources. In Jesus' abundant name, amen.

Thought

In what situation today can you practice asking the Holy Spirit for His understanding and wisdom?

Group Discussion

1. What situations in your past have you thought little of?
2. What did the Lord do in the midst of that to expand your thinking about Him or His promises?
3. Given this verse comes from the book of Job and a larger context of a believer in a season of suffering, what impact does that realization have on your own suffering seasons?

DAY 3

Longing for Real Life

When You send Your breath [or Spirit], they are created, and You renew the face of the earth.

—Psalm 104:30

One of the remarkable things that stands out to me about the Holy Spirit is that He is precise. He is sent for a specific purpose. He is an agent of change, renewal, and redemption—that could look like fire at Pentecost, setting the faith of the earliest believers aflame; or it could look like rushing waters from Revelation, sweeping everything downstream that has not been tightly anchored to Him. He can come in as the consolation of the persecuted, the healing of the afflicted, or the resurrection of the dead.

He embodies the power of love but not as a nameless, faceless force. That He is an actual person is a hard concept to grasp, but we take this on faith to be true. And when you encounter Him—when you spend time in His presence—as John Wesley said, our hearts get warm. They are breathed back into life and light. He is a real person.

You see, breath indicates speech; speech indicates intelligence and an identity. It shows that there is an identity with ability and a desire to act. It means there is thought and character. Being alive means there is an ability to reproduce; and when the Holy Spirit comes, children, not slaves, are born. Relationships are restored. The hearts of fathers are turned to their children and children return to their parents in obedience and honor. Families are healed.

The Holy Spirit reverses the curse of entropy, of chaos. He renews to counterbalance the fallen state of this world that is headed for destruction. He creates, recreates, and makes us new over and over again. He is that good! His mercies are indeed new every morning (see Lamentations 3:22–23).

We need that real life. We need warmth and promise. We need to see the force of His beauty because so much of this world is ugly. We need the Lord to send His breath so that we might be created afresh to experience renewal. We want Him to reproduce His life in our hearts. We want to be shown what delights Him so that we might pursue that instead of what we think is best. We long for Him to reverse the curses spoken over us. We need His truth to cancel out the lies we've believed. We hope for absolute truth that shows us the reality of springtime in the middle of winter. We want be restored to hope and trust more fully in the promises of God.

This is all possible because fresh creation still happens when He is present. He is the spring following the long, barren winter. He is the strength of God, exhaled from heaven for hope, for good, and for nourishment. He is the essence of life, the very wholeness of God. He is life; He counteracts and conquers death. Life is the opposite of death, so when the Holy Spirit comes, there is healing and things come back to life.

And God gets the glory.

Prayer

Come, Holy Spirit. Fill me with real life. Let me see the force with which You are renewing this earth, my life, and my heart. Put Your truth in me so that I may be set free to live in life and wholeness. Conquer the feeling of death in my life, and I will be careful to give You all the glory. In Jesus' name, amen.

Thought

Where are you witnessing the Holy Spirit breathing renewal into your life, or into those close to you?

Group Discussion

1. What have you seen as the difference between your own creation and the creation work of God in your life?
2. Do you believe the Holy Spirit will still reverse the curse of chaos that exists in this world? Why or why not?
3. What effect does giving the Holy Spirit identity as a person—not just a force—have on your faith?

DAY 4

How He Teaches

> You sent Your good Spirit to instruct them. You did not withhold Your manna from their mouths, and You gave them water for their thirst.
>
> —Nehemiah 9:20

The word that comes to me here is *provision.* Fathers are meant to provide for their children, and that is what our heavenly Father is doing through the Holy Spirit. He doesn't withhold to punish. He doesn't deny His children so that they will behave better. He doesn't try and teach them a lesson through fear, wrath, sickness, or death. Love doesn't punish. Love instructs.

This verse reminds us not only who God is, but how He operates. In context, Nehemiah is helping a broken people remember that their God is like no other. He is their heavenly Father and He has not abandoned His children. He doesn't need to be coerced or manipulated into giving. He is good, so He gives what we need.

There are times when it seems like God is withholding for a reason. Perhaps there is a reason He knows that we can't understand. Here, Nehemiah seeks to counsel the returned remnant that the same One who could do what he or she needed in the past is promising to do it again. He is faithful. Also, He isn't doing the bare minimum—even when we can't sense His presence, see Him act, or feel His touch.

Nehemiah was a man who'd risked a lucrative career in global politics to fulfill his call to rebuild Jerusalem. In the eyes of the world and culture, it seems like a pretty lousy trade-off. Yet, it feels to me like Nehemiah is daring us to trust that the Holy Spirit will do again what only He can do—provide for His children in the wasteland.

I've faced starvation of the soul, so I know how hard it is to keep reaching out for God's provision. I've looked death in the face, and there have been times when I haven't wanted to believe He will again fulfill His promises.

Even through these times, though, I couldn't believe the good Spirit of my Father was keeping something from me to punish me. Nearly every time, I've found that He was keeping me from something I wasn't ready for or wasn't right for me. When I looked back, I could see there was still so much abundance around me. I might not have had what I thought I wanted, but His deeds, His actions, and His care for me taught me He provided what I needed—that's how we learn His heart.

Even if we feel the lack of His presence or provision, that is not the truth. We can choose to keep our distance, but that is not what the Holy Spirit desires. Withholding is not His preferred teaching method.

What if He wants to ask for more than what we can imagine or think? He doesn't want His children to settle for what we know or what we can expect because our perspective is so limited. His ways are greater and His thoughts are higher. Let's trust the good Spirit of God today.

Prayer

Come, Holy Spirit. Show me how good You are. Expand my thoughts to reach higher for Yours. Show me Your provision that is beyond my understanding. Feed any starvation or thirst in me with Your presence. In Jesus' name, amen.

Thought

Have you faced a time when you couldn't see what the Lord was doing, but looking back, you can see His hand of provision?

Group Discussion

1. Have you ever struggled with thinking that the Lord was using your circumstances to punish you?
2. Has the Lord proved Himself as a provider to you?
3. If you've ever felt the lack of God's presence in your life, how did you get through that and maintain your faith?

DAY 5

Corrective Lenses

> The Spirit of the LORD will rest on Him—a Spirit of wisdom and understanding, a Spirit of counsel and strength, a Spirit of knowledge and of the fear of the LORD.
>
> —Isaiah 11:2

The greatest challenge the disciples faced was only being able to see through their own eyes. While they walked with Jesus, they didn't yet have the power to see things His way. Occasionally they got it; there was that time the Father revealed to Peter that Jesus was the Messiah. Other times they experienced life as Jesus lived it—able to do the things He did as part of His mission to set the captives free.

They struggled to grasp the hard thing: His plan to die on the cross and be raised again in three days. Yet, they stayed with Him even after the infamous statement of, "You will have to eat my flesh and drink my blood" (see John 6:53–58). However, God's plan requires more than just dogged devotion. Logic and reason are not enough to sort it out because it completely defies the natural order.

The Spirit explains these unsearchable, unknowable, and make-no-earthly-sense kinds of things. Without the Holy Spirit empowering Him to obedience, Jesus might have ended up like a skittish horse at the starting gate. He could have balked or never run. He wouldn't have finished or won His race. If that had happened, we would be worse off than when we started.

The Holy Spirit comes to us so we, too, can do things that defy the natural order. Faith in Christ itself defies logic, but once you are there, you know there is no other truth that will make sense of this life.

Jesus stated in John 10:10 that He came so we could live in abundance. But we can't do that unless our vision is perfected. Our sin (past and present), lies we believe, and wounds inflicted upon us cloud how we see. We might be wise in our own eyes, but that ends up making us pretty nearsighted. The Holy Spirit has been sent to rest in us because we need to see differently than we used to, as well as beyond what others see and believe. The Holy Spirit has to give us God's vision, which is long-term. We need Him to clear out the splinters and logs so we can see things His way. He fills us with Himself—full to the brim of knowledge—so we can learn to see things through His eyes.

With the Holy Spirit counseling us, teaching us day by day, moment by moment, He elevates our mental capacity. Our ability to process thoughts and to discern what is happening is enhanced. The more we ask Him, and the more we lean into Him as the Spirit of Wisdom, the more He renews and transforms our minds to be like Christ's. We will see what others can't or won't. We won't just see problems. With the Holy Spirit guiding us, we will see the solutions spheres of influence need.

The victorious life in Christ is the Holy Spirit guiding, teaching, and correcting us so we may walk the path Jesus paved. It is a lifelong journey, but He cheers each baby step on because, truly, each baby step starts to add up. He gives us the insight to see where we are going so we will reach a point one day where He can stop us to take a breath, then He lifts our heads to see just how far we've come.

Prayer

Come, Holy Spirit, and show me how far I've come from who I was before You came into my heart. Teach me Your ways and guide me in all Your truth. Give me Your strength to keep walking. In Jesus' name, amen.

Thought

What could the Holy Spirit be trying to clear out of your heart, mind, or life to be able to see through His eyes?

Group Discussion

1. Have you ever experienced someone in the church who had a lack of insight? What was the result?
2. Have you ever had a lack of insight? How did it affect others?
3. How have you seen the transformation of mind-sets by the power of the Holy Spirit? What were the results?

DAY 6

Cleansing Flow

> I will also sprinkle clean water on you, and you will be clean. I will cleanse you from all your impurities and all your idols. I will give you a new heart and put a new spirit within you; I will remove your heart of stone and give you a heart of flesh. I will place my Spirit within in you and cause you to follow My statutes and carefully observe My ordinances.
>
> —Ezekiel 36:25–27

So much of our faith is centered on the simple acts of washing and cleaning. The hugely symbolic and eternity-changing act of washing clean is something we do everyday with our bodies and many other things, like a sink full of dirty dishes. Right now, they are calling out to me to come and clean them with hot water and dish soap so they can be fully baptized by the dishwasher, to come out sparkly clean on the other side. This example is an ordinary act of the everyday, but in the hands of God, and when done to us, the ordinary takes on life-altering possibilities.

We are all dishes of some sort too. The Bible calls them "vessels," or "jars of clay." I wonder if this verse from Ezekiel is what Paul had in mind when he wrote his second letter to Timothy, describing, "If anyone cleanses himself from these things [which are dishonorable—disobedient, sinful], he will be a vessel for honor, sanctified, [set apart for a special purpose and] useful to the Master, prepared for every good work" (2:21 AMP). It takes cleansing to get us to full use. By His grace, He will do the cleaning all on His own.

All of us have been clogged with junk; and all of us need the open-heart-and-soul surgery. He has to take out what is inside, but He doesn't just wash it and put it back. He puts back something entirely new. He puts in a new heart—one that can operate at higher levels—fueled by the renewable resource of His love, received by His own Spirit within us.

This is the lightning bolt into Frankenstein's creation, without the resulting monster. It's the opposite, actually. We were monsters; and now, through a new heart, redeemed human spirit, and the indwelling of the one and only Holy Spirit, we are the gorgeous creatures we were meant and born to be. Truly, though, at this moment of eternal renewal, we are but newborns. We have to grow up into this new heart, learning from the Holy Spirit inside us and inside our community of faith.

We need to remain open vessels—clean dishes ready to serve the good-tasting fruit He has for the world. And to stay that way, we need regular washing. We need regular immersion. The Holy Spirit is the agent for that. He is ready to refresh us. All we need to do is ask Him to wash us clean again, to refuel our tanks with His love, and use His power to clean us up so we can be ready to be used by Him, for His purposes today.

Prayer

Come, Holy Spirit. I need Your loving, gentle touch to wash off the grit and grime of life in this world. I've come to You to give me what I need right now, and welcome immersion in Your presence to renew me to health, wholeness, and purpose. I open my hands and heart to You to make me clean for Your holy use. In Jesus' name, amen.

Thought

Are you in any way afraid to expose your heart to the cleansing ministry of the Holy Spirit?

Group Discussion

1. Do you have a baptism story that moved you?
2. Do you remember your own baptism?
3. What do you think it means to be baptized in the Holy Spirit?

DAY 7

A Vision to Encourage

So he answered me, "This is the word of the LORD to Zerubbabel: 'Not by strength or by might, but by My Spirit,' says the LORD of Hosts. 'What are you, great mountain? Before Zerubbabel you will become a plain. And he will bring out the capstone accompanied by shouts of: Grace, grace to it!'"

—Zechariah 4:6–7

I love the prophet Zechariah. I don't understand everything in the book that contains his name, but there are some awe-inspiring visions to meditate upon. My personal love for him comes from the fact that he came to prophesy not just the future, but to encourage. He was speaking to a despairing people, but especially to one of the leaders over the returning exiles coming back after the Babylonian captivity. I love to encourage, exhort, and prophesy what I hear from God's heart over people too. I love bringing a word of hope and light. To see the Holy Spirit refresh a weary soul with a grace-filled word is no better high. I identify with what friends of mine say: "We are hope dealers!"

Hope needs a foundation. In this verse, the hope Zechariah is communicating is based on one thing and one thing only: dependence. In order for mountains to fall before this leader, or any leader or believer, we have to come to the place of knowing we are not capable of making miracles happen. This verse is clear: not by our strength, our understanding, or even our expectations on things will mountains collapse and the capstones of grace emerge. It is only by the Spirit—the Holy Spirit of God—doing what only He can do.

It is good to remember how small we are, but this verse is saying so much more. It is saying we should remember and focus on how much bigger the Holy Spirit is than the mountains in our lives. He is so big the mountains tremble before Him and He easily makes them flat land. He will be the new foundation stone called *grace*.

The things of God are done by God. Only He can do them. How many of us have tried to make God's plan happen for us on our timing and in our own strength? It usually ends badly, resulting in burnout. It is a daily practice in prayer for me to say, "Lord, I don't understand. I am not going to try and understand but trust in Your grace and will for me." It is in this very act of dependence that the Spirit says, "I got this!"

We each have an assignment, a good future He wants us to live into. There are things we hold onto—broken relationships, lies, physical circumstances—standing in the way. We've all tried our best to get over, around, or go through them, but it will never be complete when we go at it alone. This vision was given to encourage us to trust and ask the Spirit of the living God to do what only He can do.

God graciously gives me chances to step aside so He can make the mountain flat land for me to walk across. It rarely happens the way I think it will (or when I think it should), but that leaves me in awe because it is always better and a much more powerful way to get it done. His way makes me thankful. That is how I find I am more dependent on Him, as I acknowledge His power over my life. That is why I stand and shout: Won't He do it?

Prayer

Come, Holy Spirit, because I am dependent on You doing what only You can. I surrender to Your grace, Your timing, and seek Your encouragement as I face my day.

Help me to see You at work. I am ever grateful for Your consistency on my behalf. In Jesus' mighty name, amen.

Thought

What mountains do you want to see God move, and how can you surrender them to Him today?

Group Discussion

1. How do you see dependence creating hope in your life?
2. What things of God are you trying to make happen in your own strength or power? What could you let go of in order to see more of the Holy Spirit working in your life?
3. Do you trust the Holy Spirit to do what He promises—and even above and beyond?

DAY 8

Filling the Low Places

"I baptize you with water for repentance, but the One who is coming after me is more powerful than I. I am not worthy to remove His sandals. He Himself will baptize you with the Holy Spirit and fire."

—Matthew 3:11

When water comes in, it goes to the low places first. I know this because of some massive flooding events in my home in Houston in 2014, 2015, and 2016. On all three occasions, the drainage system in our backyard couldn't keep up and our pool overflowed. Our house sits a little lower than our backyard, and that water had to go somewhere. Despite doors and walls, it came in and covered the downstairs of our house. We fixed the problem, finally, the third time the water came in. The solution, as it turned out, was simple. And the timing couldn't have been better because just as my older girls and I were praying for God to help us, my husband was walking around the house to drill three holes in the bottom of our fence. All the water drained out of the backyard and stopped coming into our house. We haven't had water in the house since, even during Hurricane Harvey. Miracles come in all shapes and sizes, including six-foot engineers with power tools.

When I think of baptism, I picture this flooding. I picture the living water rushing in, unstoppable and going to the lowest parts first. We are literally immersed in the grace of God at the moment of salvation. The baptism of the Holy Spirit, which can be a separate experience, allows the power of His presence to rush into our souls and bodies. It can result in unique expressions of joy as we let the Holy Spirit bubble in and up through our beings.

At Aldersgate, John Wesley met His Savior and was baptized in the waters of grace. At Fetter's Lane, he had an experience where his heart was infused with the very presence of God Himself and was launched into his history-changing ministry, which birthed a new movement and multiple denominations. The nineteenth-century evangelist Charles Finney described his experience as "waves of liquid love." Now that's some flooding!

I've been saved since I was fourteen years old. Even having been saved for thirty years now, I've known the power of the Holy Spirit in my life for just a few of those years. I felt the Lord before my own encounter with the Holy Spirit, but since then I feel more solid, more peaceful, and more assured God loves me and is for me than I did before. There are still times I need to be reminded of the power that raised Christ from the dead that lives in me. I need the confirmation and purification to do the things He calls me to do (which is most everything in my life).

Asking for the Holy Spirit baptism is at once an act of obedience and surrender. It is putting down our ways and understanding to choose God's way. And that refreshing water rushes into the lowest places first. Maybe there is a dry quality to your heart. If your spirit feels restless or if it's taking a long nap, it's time to ask. If your heart is hard or you are weary of the trials of this life, it's time to ask. If you just came off a mountaintop, it's time to ask.

As the people of God, it is time to ask for more. Don't just settle for water on the first floor; ask Him to fill you up to the rafters and overflow out the chimney.

He won't hold back Himself from you when you ask for Him. Whether you feel anything or not isn't the point.

The point is to ask Him to come in and fill you with His presence so your life can be filled with His. Trust that when you ask, He will rush in to those low places with all the blessing you need.

Prayer

Come, Holy Spirit, and fill me with Yourself. Fill my low places, but don't stop there. Fill me all the way up with Your presence, Lord. In Jesus' name, amen.

Thought

What would your life be like if you experienced the power of God working in and through you every day?

Group Discussion

1. Have you ever heard a story about the movement of the Holy Spirit that has concerned you or made you skeptical about another's experience?
2. Do you believe the Holy Spirit still anoints people with the gifts and experiences like we see in Scripture?
3. If you've experienced the power of the Holy Spirit for yourself, and you are comfortable, share how it has changed your walk of faith.

DAY 9

Spoken For

> Don't worry about how or what you should speak. For you will be given what to say at that hour, because you are not speaking, but the Spirit of your Father is speaking through you.
>
> —Matthew 10:19–20

Who is the Holy Spirit, really? The short answer is: the indwelling presence of God. This is a phrase I don't connect with immediately; I am one who needs detail. Thankfully, the Lord made a way in His Word for people like me; He gets very specific and descriptive. This is one of those verses that give me a little jolt in my gut. Not only are we sons and daughters, heirs, and coheirs with Christ, but we are armed with the Word.

When it comes to knowing what to say, we don't have to sweat it. The Spirit of our true Father will make sure we have the words, or He will stand between us to make our faltering words hit their mark.

There is an inborn authority with the word *father*. As a mother, I have my own authority, but there are situations where my girls just aren't listening. When I ask my husband to step in, there is a remarkable shift. When he speaks in that dad voice, suddenly the message I've been trying to repeatedly communicate sinks in.

Jesus knew we need not only power but also wisdom. We need help knowing what the Father is doing and how to communicate it. It was the fulfillment of Jesus' words when Peter stood up and delivered one of the most thorough and compelling sermons of all time in the temple courts. That only happened through the empowerment of the Holy Spirit after Jesus finished His work, went to glory, and the tongue of fire rested on Peter's shoulder.

The reality Jesus speaks into being here is the removal of our own understanding or need to worry about what to say, how to say it, or what we sound like. He put Himself in us; He will be in us and give us what we need in the moment! I take this for granted and tend to sweat over what I am going to say and how it sounds after the fact. Many of us are deathly afraid of public speaking. We don't tap into this gift nearly as often, if ever, as we should.

Yet the promise is right here! We don't have to worry about what others say or what we might have to say back—the Father will speak back through us! We have access, through the Spirit of our Father, to all the knowledge and mystery—the deep things He wants to reveal to us and through us. The real kicker is that the thoughts and words we have access to will only make this world a better place!

The Holy Spirit can pull grace from His heart and put it into our mouths. We don't have to have anxiety, but we do have to ask Him for help. The more we practice this surrender, the more we learn about Him and how faithful, kind, gentle, and merciful He is. Even when we speak incorrectly, He can turn that into an opportunity to connect to another's heart. He makes all things work out for the good of those who love Him and are called according to His purposes, even when the words don't come out right.

I challenge you to practice accessing the heart of the Father for yourself and others today. Before you speak, to converse or respond, just pause. Whisper in your heart, *My Father, My Papa, My Abba-Daddy, what would you have me say here?*

Prayer

Come, Holy Spirit. I ask You to put Your words in my mouth today. May the words of my mouth and the meditations of my heart be acceptable in Your sight and bless others through Your power. In Jesus' name, amen.

Thought

With Jesus' promise in your heart and trust in the power of the Holy Spirit, what can you speak out that you might be holding in or hesitating to believe He will make come out right?

Group Discussion

1. Attentive listening is paying more attention to what the other person is saying than preparing your own response. How might employing attentive listening give the Holy Spirit room to give you the right words to say at the right time?
2. Have you been the right person, speaking the right word, at the right time? What kind of impact did that have on the hearer? What kind of impact did it have on you?
3. Does this verse give you any confidence, or does fear or hesitation still give you pause at the thought of speaking truth to power?

DAY 10

Spirit in Action

And the angel answered and said unto her, The Holy Ghost shall come upon thee, and the power of the Highest shall overshadow thee: therefore also that holy thing which shall be born of thee shall be called the Son of God.

—Luke 1:35 KJV

The word we translate "come upon," has several meanings. I love to study the original text because it gives us a greater picture of what the writers meant with the words they chose. It's the verb *eperchomai*—this is the Holy Spirit in action. This is what happens when He enters our space, time, and bodies. It means to arrive and to overtake. Interestingly, one of the root words of this word expands the picture for us even further. It describes the action of the Holy Spirit here as "to come into being; to arise and come forth." It can mean the power of God on display being established and able to be known in our natural, physical world.

The power of God is always on display in heaven. In heaven, there are no limits as to how God can be experienced. But on earth, there are indeed limiters, even inside of our own bodies. That's why we so often call how the Lord operates "miracles." I believe what we call miracles are really just the Lord's normal way of operating. What we see as impossible isn't hard for the Lord! It took a miracle for Mary to get pregnant, but I don't believe it was hard for the Holy Spirit to overtake her to create Jesus in her womb.

Saints in all generations have done mighty things that testify to God's power to accomplish what He wants, and to deliver His children. They were overtaken by His power and could do what they normally couldn't. This happens even more so since Jesus' promise that we would do greater things via the Holy Spirit coming on Pentecost.

It's not surprising that God can do wondrous and mighty acts. It is His standard operating procedure to be awesome and infinitely able to do whatever He wants according to His loving and just nature.

If we are being honest, we have to admit, Mary was a nobody. She belonged to a people whose promised land was now occupied by another. She wasn't even from Jerusalem, but a backwater country. She had nothing to offer; her only contribution was half the genetic material required to create a person (and an imperfect set of genes at that). Yet, God saw something in her—faith. Faith is the soil of miracles. What we see as nothing to offer, God, the Holy Spirit, sees as an opportunity to demonstrate His might. So, He condescended to her. He came upon her and created Emmanuel, the long-promised Messiah. He did it through a family whose genealogy didn't matter anymore. He fulfilled His promise at a time when the chosen ones had long since grown weary of waiting. Yet, since He promised to do it, He did it. He acted in power and might, by His Spirit alone.

He doesn't need us to help Him, but I believe His preferred way of working is through those who are willing. It doesn't matter what they look like, where they are from, or what they are capable of in their own strength. The Spirit will come when we ask and when we are open to it. Mary was ready. She was ready to be the vessel for the promise to come through. Are you a willing child today? Are you open for the Spirit to come and use His power to help you, your spouse, your children, and your church?

Prayer

Come, Holy Spirit, in Your power and whatever way You choose. I desire to be a willing vessel to carry Your promises to the world. I desire to be Your willing child. I know You are able and I know You can. I am open to be used for miracles today, Lord. In Jesus' name, amen.

Thought

Is there anything in the way of the Holy Spirit coming upon you in power today?

Group Discussion

1. If the church asked for the power of the Holy Spirit today, do you think we would get it?
2. Dream for a moment. What would things in our lives, churches, and cities look like if the people of God would access the power of God to communicate to the world?
3. Have you ever experienced the power of the Holy Spirit for yourself?

DAY 11

The Spirit in Plain Sight

There was a man in Jerusalem whose name was Simeon. This man was righteous and devout, looking forward to Israel's consolation [Messiah's coming], and the Holy Spirit was on him.

—Luke 2:25

When I'm tempted to condemn myself for not being devout or righteous enough, I am relieved to remember Simeon was old. He was an old man with a lot of practice in looking for the Messiah—decades of practice and years spent in God's presence. It gives me something to look forward to, that possibly someday one of my children or grandchildren will describe me like Simeon. It will surely be after I'm really old.

We get caught in the thought that the Holy Spirit came on the scene at Pentecost. We attribute that moment like His incarnation—his manger. The truth is, He's been around and is as prevalent in the story of God in our history since we first read about Him in Genesis. He's been active; we've seen Him move throughout the Old Testament. Now in the coming of the long-sought Messiah, He gives someone ready to see it the eyes to be a witness.

The Holy Spirit has come to help us understand God's thoughts and desires. He always brings us back around to Jesus because Christ is the image of the invisible God we need the help to see. Who better to help us but God Himself? He isn't just a messenger, but the very anointing oil that opens our spiritual senses to the presence of God in our midst.

Simeon made a life of looking. He was a witness—a seeker. He was ready and willing to connect with God, which is why I believe the Holy Spirit was so unmistakable to Him. The more we practice something, the better we get at it, similar to muscle memory in sports. Simeon's spiritual muscles were so strong, he could recognize when the Holy Spirit was telling him something. Because of that pursuit of a relationship with God in the Holy Spirit, Simeon was rewarded for his faithfulness: laying eyes on the precious Savior who would bring about the reconciliation of heaven and earth.

My middle daughter has often asked me how to know the difference between her own voice, the voice of the enemy, and the voice of God. I've told her simply that the Holy Spirit only speaks good things. We might not always understand them at the time, but His words are loving and peaceful, even when He is correcting us. He shows us, in living color, what the promises are in His Word. That is simple, but sometimes simple is best. God is love, so that is what He speaks and what He brings to us.

For our part in this, we must have expectant hearts and open eyes, like Simeon. The more we look, seek, and track the work of what the Holy Spirit is doing in our lives, the more we see it. The Holy Spirit doesn't play hide-and-seek. Jesus didn't give Himself in pieces, and neither does the Holy Spirit. He is out there in plain sight. We, like Simeon, have to practice looking for Him. He wants us to be excited about seeing how He is bringing the full picture of God into view—by the life, death, and resurrection of Jesus and how that applies here and now.

Prayer

Come, Holy Spirit, and open my heart. I want my sense of You to be as strong as my seeing, hearing, touching, tasting, and smelling. Lord, work through me to prepare me to see Your work of consolation in this world. In the name of Jesus Christ, amen.

Thought

Reflect on a time when the Lord, like Simeon, gave you eyes to see His promises.

Group Discussion

1. We need Simeons in the church. Does your church have someone, either now or in the past, who was clearly in touch with the Holy Spirit and encouraged others to be?
2. What have you seen the Holy Spirit do in your life or the life of another?
3. Can you say right now that your heart is open to witnessing a promise or answer to prayer?

DAY 12

Inviting the Spirit-Wind to Blow

"The wind blows where it pleases, and you hear its sound, but you don't know where it comes from or where it is going. So it is with everyone born of the Spirit."

—John 3:8

The day I looked at this verse, I was struggling with accepting myself, especially as how God sees me. I wrote this in my journal: *I acutely feel the tension between my human and my divine self. Neither rules—they are both present and at work. I need you, Lord, to help me balance the good way to walk, and to stop questioning myself and my worth in You. I want to just go with the flow but I think—I overthink. How do I rest and work in You, Lord?*

In this verse, Jesus gives this enigmatic gem to Nicodemus, a man deep in the ministry of God and a high-ranking member of the Jewish ruling class. Nicodemus knew the law, but still came to Jesus because something was missing. He came under the cover of night, perhaps out of shame he couldn't solve his inner need on his own. The day I read this verse, I was also coming to the Lord under the cloak of shame of my own self-doubt. Nicodemus wanted to know how to know God, and so did I.

This verse is not a ringer that helps us grasp the Holy Spirit. The Spirit is not subject to us, but only goes where the Father sends Him. He partners with the will of God alone to reveal the person and work of Jesus. We can't tell Him what to do, where to go, who to save, or when to do it. We can only petition our King, asking in humble worship. We are to invite the wind to blow in our direction. We can make a tunnel for Him to blow through, but He is still going to determine when, where, and how (if at all) He will blow through it.

Maybe that was why Jesus gave Nicodemus such a head-scratcher. Jesus could see the Pharisees thought that who they were or how well they followed religious rule meant they could tell God what to do. But human perfection is never the key to answered prayer, even if I live like that sometimes. Perhaps that's what got me to the mental state I was in the day I wrote that prayer. I know I can't tell God what to do! But at the same time, in all my efforts to be right, I'd created this dynamic between my heart and mind that left me unstable in my thinking, not remembering how to find my rest.

The solution to this instability is surrender. I've found my heart position and attitude in prayer determines what I get out of it. Perhaps Nicodemus wasn't coming so much for answers or solutions, but for wisdom. Perhaps he realized this in his conversation with Jesus, looking at things from a different angle to understand.

My goal in coming to the Holy Spirit can't start with my wants and desires. Remembering who He is breaks the back of my pride and opens the door for the fresh wind of the Holy Spirit to blow through. Like that first cold front blowing through Texas after a long, hot summer, He restores my soul. In letting Him be the Lord and humbly asking for His presence, the Spirit comes. Anything less leaves us with nothing to stand on. In surrender, we remember He is the solid rock on which we stand.

Prayer

Come, Holy Spirit, and blow aside anything in the way of Your refreshing, reassuring presence. Remind me who You are and enable me to stand in confidence in

Your finished work and desire to be with me. In Jesus' name, amen.

Thought

Do you harbor any doubts, insecurities, pride, fear, or traditional way of thinking that gets in the way of the Holy Spirit blowing in and through your life?

Group Discussion

1. Have you been through a time in your faith when you've struggled with doubt, especially self-doubt? How did the Lord speak into that and remind you of who you are in Him?
2. Has religion ever left you dry and dusty in your soul?
3. Share what you've discovered in seeking a fresh movement of the Holy Spirit in your life.

DAY 13

Eternal Thirst-Quencher

On the last and most important day of the festival, Jesus stood up and cried out, "If anyone is thirsty, he should come to Me and drink! The one who believes in Me, as the Scripture has said, will have streams of living water flow from deep within him." He said this about the Spirit. Those who believed in Jesus were going to receive the Spirit, for the Spirit had not yet been received because Jesus had not yet been glorified.

—John 7:37–39

This scripture finds us at the pinnacle of the Feast of Tabernacles, the very last day. Much like the cauldron at the opening of the Olympic Games is lit, Jesus chooses this moment to stand up and proclaim who He is. He was heralding publicly in front of thousands that the Messiah had come—and He was it. Imagine the electricity in the air! Imagine the charge His disciples must have felt hearing these words!

His imagery of the Holy Spirit as living water is critical for such a barren, dry land. People knew about being thirsty. Think of His conversation with the Samaritan woman, who went to the well, especially at midday.

The context of this passage is important to understand the role of the Holy Spirit Jesus was describing. At the Feast of Tabernacles, water was poured out daily at the altar to remind everyone of the water God miraculously provided for a thirsty Israel in the wilderness. This represented the people's physical thirst, but Jesus takes it up an eternal level. Here, He calls out that we are more than just one part. Like the image of the Trinity we are made in, we are three parts: spirit, soul, and body (and all thirst). He is the eternal Thirst-Quencher for every part of us.

When our souls are dry, we physically lag. When our spirits are thirsty, our minds suffer. When we are outside and get overheated, not only do our wells of energy run dry but our spiritual reserves are spent. There is nothing left to move us forward, no matter how willing our hearts and spirits are; if our bodies suffer, so does the rest of us.

We must be refilled. Our thirst, regardless of the origin in mind, body, or spirit, drives us to the well (or hose or faucet). It all relates together.

Not only do we need to be poured into, but we have to complete that eternal water cycle. We need to pour out into others to keep the streams of living water moving. We need to give out what we've been given by God. My husband would see it more as a pipeline than a cycle. Pipelines, in order to be the best vessels, need to be open on both ends and clear in the middle; so should we be in order for the Holy Spirit to come in and flow out, with nothing holding Him back. We are to be quenched to overflowing, and then pouring into others. The process is meant to be a constant coming in and going out.

There are times when that river is at flash-flood stage, and other seasons when it is calm, where people can come and find rest. Yet, always the water flows.

Prayer

Come, Holy Spirit, and flow into my heart. Refresh me and quench my thirst for You in mind, body, and soul. Wash away anything that blocks Your loving presence, not just to remember Your promises but to be reassured of Your goodness and mercy. Let that hope flow through me into others. In Jesus' name, amen.

Thought

Imagine you were one of the crowd hearing Jesus' words. What stands out to you the most?

Group Discussion

1. How does Jesus declaring Himself as both bread and water speak to our deepest needs?
2. What do you picture as the way the Holy Spirit overflows into this world? What kind of vessel do you imagine?
3. What ways is the Holy Spirit using you as the vessel to quench thirst or satisfy hunger in this world?

DAY 14

A Good, Perfect, and Pleasing Order

"If you love Me, you will keep My commands. And I will ask the Father, and He will give you another Counselor to be with you forever. He is the Spirit of truth. The world is unable to receive Him because it doesn't see Him or know Him. But you do know Him, because He remains with you and will be in you."

—John 14:15–17

Jesus asked the Father for more than He could give us while on earth. Knowing His limitations (those He willingly placed on Himself), He asked His Father for more. He asked for a better deal. Most of us might think Jesus in physical form would be the ultimate, but the Lord, in His infinite wisdom, knew it was not. He came so there could be even greater intimacy. He had to demonstrate what was possible so there could be more.

He knew the Father would give more because it was His will too. That was always part of their plan, to make available more and better resources. It's essentially this: the Holy Spirit is a trade up from Jesus!

There is a perfect order to it all. Jesus was only a temporary solution, a stopgap. He is the way that restores us to right relationship to the Father. Jesus had to come first to build the bridge across the vast waterway of sin. Jesus is the only and necessary ferry from the World of the Lost to the Island of the Found. The world is lost because it can't receive Christ—it won't receive Him. The world misses Jesus because they aren't looking; they aren't seeking. They don't want any more than they know. We are the found because we seek, we hunger, and we desire more.

The Holy Spirit was the more, but He couldn't come and knock on the doors of our hearts until Jesus completed His work. The Trinity did it step by step, without failing to dot an "I" or cross a "T." The Trinity wouldn't leave anything about this to chance; no point of failure, no matter how small, would be allowed. So Jesus lived. He died. He rose again. He ascended to the right hand of the Father. Then it was the Holy Spirit's turn. He set fire to the disciples and made them apostles.

Their ability to set fire to the world with the gospel of Christ was only possible with His tender, powerful, and indwelling presence. Yet, He had to be patient and wait His turn. The trade up was only possible when all the boxes were checked and the dotted line was signed with the precious blood of the Lamb.

Order is not what I always want from the Holy Spirit. I want instant gratification and intervention, especially when my circumstances are frustrating and painful. It is in those times I feel Him reminding me His will is always good and it is always pleasing—the very best option for me and for many. Plus, His will is perfect. His plans leave no point of failure. His plans are not a house of cards that could come falling down at any moment. His plans are only secure and stable, built on the solid rock of Christ.

Are we able to trust Him enough to wait for His trade up to our thoughts and plans? Even if the answer is no, He graciously gives an extra dose of supernatural strength and faith, enabling us to be empowered to wait for His good, pleasing, and perfect plan to be fulfilled in our lives.

Prayer

Come, Holy Spirit. Fill me with the hope of Your good, perfect, and pleasing order for my life—plans that will bring a hope and future to me and to many. Let my heart be at rest in Yours so Your way can be made complete in me. In Jesus' name, amen.

Thought

What temporal problem do you need an eternal solution to in your life?

Group Discussion

1. Would you rather have Jesus in the flesh or the Holy Spirit indwelling?
2. Is there any part of the plan of salvation you've struggled to understand?
3. Share a time when you chose instant gratification over waiting on the Lord.

DAY 15

The Voice of Truth

"But the Counselor, the Holy Spirit—the Father will send Him in My name—will teach you all things and remind you of everything I have told you."

—John 14:26

While taking a final my sophomore year in college, I needed help with an answer. I remember the moment clearly. I was drawing a blank—almost sure I'd never learned the material. Then suddenly, there was a distinct moment of clarity when I knew the answer. It seemed to come from within me, but not really from me. It seemed to spring fully formed from my head onto the paper. I sat in awe for a few seconds before I finished the rest of the test.

That experience revealed to me what real truth feels like. It was a "knowing," crystal clear and unwavering. I don't mean what feels true, but truth with a capital *T*. We all have our individual truths, those beliefs and experiences that filter the way we see the world. Sometimes, however, those aren't a real absolute, but rather our understanding of the way the world works, or because of a situation in our past—how we relate to it. My truth is easily influenced and twisted by others. You could call that being flexible, even teachable. However, real truth is not negotiable. There was a fifteen-year period in my life when I didn't understand the difference between absolute truth and someone else's personal truth. My soul bears the scars of that season and my lack of knowledge of truth.

The Holy Spirit comes to us to teach us not just truths about Jesus, but the truth of Jesus—who He is, what He has done, and why it is imperative to live His way. There is plenty of mystery in our faith, and plenty to wonder over. Even so, that mystery is grounded in the absolute—personified in Jesus Christ—as a reflection of the invisible God. It is the responsibility and mission of the Holy Spirit to ground us in that absolute, to teach us and remind us of Jesus. Real truth is not relative or subjective—it is what it is and we know it at a visceral level. No amount of validation, justification, liberalization, generational teaching, preferences, or cultural norms can change the absolute truth. It is up to us to go deep, and to go past what we have learned to seek the real truth of the revealed truth in Scripture.

God the Holy Spirit wants us to have moments of clarity—experiences we know are real and true. He wants us to know Jesus and make our understanding clear and in line with Him. That involves feeling, but also growing into it as an intentional process. We must be diligent in discerning right from wrong, as well as being teachable in His hands. It may take time to work out what He is revealing and apply it to our lives, to break down and through relative truths. The Holy Spirit has to loosen their hold. The truth sometimes has to bubble up from such a deep place that it takes a long time.

The unique and beautiful grace of a relationship with the Holy Spirit is that He is constantly soaking us in the truth. He doesn't reveal cold, hard facts, but warm, life-restoring love. The more time we spend with Him, the more we are exposed to the absolute of Christ. The more we let Him teach and remind us of Christ, the more liberated we become to live as He intended. The Holy Spirit is the most stable structure to build upon. As the classic hymn says, "On Christ, the solid Rock, I stand; all other ground is sinking sand."

Prayer

Come, Holy Spirit, to teach me new things about Jesus and about Yourself today. Reveal the truth to my spirit and let it sink into my mind, heart, and body. Remind me of Jesus' words throughout my day and let me live according to the deep truth of Your counsel. In Jesus' name, amen.

Thought

What hope for revelation do you carry to better understand what the Lord is doing in your circumstances?

Group Discussion

1. What mountains of your own perception and understanding has the Holy Spirit shaken up in your life?
2. Have you experienced moments of clarity where you felt the truth as much as you knew it?
3. Are you open for the Holy Spirit to reveal more truth about Jesus (and, consequently, yourself) today?

DAY 16

Remaining in Grace

> "When he comes, he'll expose the error of the godless world's view of sin, righteousness, and judgment: He'll show them that their refusal to believe in me is their basic sin; that righteousness comes from above, where I am with the Father, out of their sight and control."
>
> John 16:8–10 MSG

Like many college students, when I got started, I didn't think about God at all. I was raised in church, sure, but during my college years, worldly pursuits were far more interesting than religious ones. Away from home, I put my feet on holy ground just twice in four years.

In my final semester, I had to take a class I'd put off. There were only six people in it. I went to class faithfully until the last six weeks when senioritis hit. I knew when the final paper was due, so I skipped the last two weeks of class. Blissful in my ignorance, the professor moved up the due date of the final paper. I found this out, walking across campus one day, when I ran into a classmate. She informed me they'd just finished their final paper presentations that hour! I knew I was in trouble. If I didn't pass this class, I wouldn't graduate in two weeks, and then perhaps be found beaten senseless at the hands of my mother. But the worst part was I hadn't even started to write the paper!

I mustered up all the courage I had, greatly motivated by the fear of having to tell my parents. I went to the professor's office and threw myself on his mercy. He didn't let me get more than ten words out before he stopped me. I knew my doom was imminent. He asked me, "Do you know why I had a class to teach this semester? I had a class and a job because a graduating senior, that means you, registered for it. Don't bother about the paper. Go. Graduate and start your life. It's my graduation present to you. Don't come back, just go." He wanted nothing in return. So, I graduated and started my life. It would be nearly ten years before I could name what that experience was about: God's grace.

That professor saved me from my parents' wrath, but the grace of God in Jesus Christ saved me from so much more than that. The Holy Spirit is constantly teaching me what receiving true grace brings: a desire for righteousness.

Righteousness has nothing to do with me or my efforts. As Jesus says in this verse, it comes from above—out of my sight, and far beyond my understanding and possible control. Grace is the product of the love and mercy of God, while righteousness is remaining in His grace.

As the Lord determined to save me, He also determined the Holy Spirit would be with me. For a start, He reminds me what sin is: a refusal to believe in Christ and believe only in myself. Before Christ, I deserved judgment, just like I deserved to fail that class. Yet, in His mercy, He stayed His hand of judgment. He chose redemption instead. The Holy Spirit waited for me. He pursued me. He acted for me, even when I had nothing to give in return. So, I focus on staying with Him, abiding in His love, and reveling in mercy. That's the best and only way I've found to right living, to experiencing the righteousness in Christ. The Holy Spirit, the embodiment of mercy, opens the door and His love keeps us moving with Him, made able to stay in a state of grace. I love Him because He saved me, but I also love Him because He is so lovable. And He made me whole, able to keep believing, and faithful.

Prayer

Come, Holy Spirit, and pour out Your open door of mercy and righteousness on my mind, heart, and soul. Enable me to rest in You. Make me laser-focused on what You give and what You have done for me. Let me trust You more and be more faithful to Your Word and will. In Jesus' name, amen.

Thought

Write down a time when you experienced the saving hand of God's grace on your life and share it with someone this week.

Group Discussion

1. Have you ever felt the horror of your sin and mistakes being exposed openly? Did you try to hide it or did you choose to own up to it?
2. Has righteousness had different meanings for you over the course of your faith journey?
3. How does it make you feel to know that God's grace isn't under your, or anyone else's control?

DAY 17

The Cure to Fear

> Jesus said to them again, "Peace to you! As the Father has sent Me, I also send you!" After saying this, He breathed on them and said, "Receive the Holy Spirit. If you forgive the sins of any, they are forgiven them; if you retain the sins of any, they are retained."
>
> —John 20:21–23

I love John's account of the first appearance of the risen Christ to the disciples. Jesus comes to them when they are in the middle of abject terror for their lives. They figured what happened to Him was going to happen to them. When you strike the shepherd, supposedly the sheep will scatter. Yet, the Lord had a different way of going about this. Even though this Shepherd was struck down, He was raised up and came for His sheep. Showing His true nature, He didn't rebuke them because they were afraid. It looks like, actually, He doesn't even seem to notice the disciples shaking in their boots. He speaks a word of peace—a word that both means soul salvation and exemption from war and violence—to calm them so they could receive something far bigger than courage. He was giving them the cure to fear.

Fear is a big deal because it is a faith-killer. For those who have known, seen, and experienced freedom in Christ, we should know better than to panic and to be afraid. Still though, there are times when I am afraid. I am worried I will let people down; it keeps me from doing what He has called me to do.

I know paralyzing fear by name. I experienced regular panic attacks for nearly a year. Yet when God has a purpose, nothing will stop it—not even this level of fear. There is a healthy, biological need for fear. We need those instinctual checks and balances to keep us alive because not every situation is safe. Spiritual fear is a different animal altogether. Because of the fall in Eden, it is rooted in us.

Jesus shows us here the provision that God has made against reacting out of spiritual fear for His children. As the apostle John wrote later in one of his sermons: "perfect love casts out [all] fear" (1 John 4:18 ESV). Even though fear has deep roots in us, in this moment of Jesus breathing on the disciples and their reception of the Holy Spirit, He reverses that part of the curse.

I believe the forty days Jesus spent with the disciples before His ascension continued this course of treatment. I see it like a continual IV drip of perfect love therapy. Fear was a part of the disciples' cultural history, as it is part of ours. Jesus wisely uses this time to kill the deadly communicable disease of fear that could kill the movement of His kingdom spreading throughout the world. The Holy Spirit all throughout the book of Acts gives believers booster shots of perfect love. He empowers them to do miraculous things, implementing the reality of Jesus' victory over sin and death.

The coming kingdom couldn't begin to manifest worldwide until the disciples were in good spiritual health. Fear can't stand up to the power of God; the more booster shots of perfect love we receive, the healthier we become. Maybe today is your day to start the healing regimen of perfect love. Ask the Holy Spirit to begin that good work in you.

Prayer

Come, Holy Spirit. Begin the process of curing me of fear so that I may regain full spiritual health and be sent to do the work in my space and time You empower me to do—to make Your kingdom and Your redemptive plan visible and permanent on this earth. In Jesus' name, amen.

Thought

Sit with the Holy Spirit for a few minutes and ask Him to reveal the things you are afraid of, and then ask Him to show you how He has overcome those fears so you may be enabled to act from faith.

Group Discussion

1. Do you come from a family history of faith or fear? Can you give an example?
2. If you struggle with anxiety, have you ever explored the root of the fear?
3. Have you ever dreamed what life would be like if you never had to be afraid of anything?

DAY 18

Right on Time

Suddenly a sound like that of a violent rushing wind came from heaven, and it filled the whole house where they were staying. And tongues, like flames of fire that were divided, appeared to them and rested on each one of them. Then they were all filled with the Holy Spirit and began to speak in different languages, as the Spirit gave them ability for speech.

—Acts 2:2–4

This should be the easiest, most straightforward depiction of the Spirit's coming. It's the most familiar, and is often used as the prototypical example of how the fullness of the Spirit enters into humanity. First, there was a violent wind-like sound. Then the fire fell. Then the Holy Spirit filled the believers and they spoke in the languages

He gave them—seems like a good plan and even a formula to follow.

I'm not a big believer in formulas when it comes to the Holy Spirit. I think He teaches us how He normally does things, but in the end, it is His choice how to make things happen. In John 3:8, we saw Jesus teach that there is no predicting when the Holy Spirit will come or what He will do. I bet all one hundred and twenty people gathered together in the upper room had no clue this was the day they would all become a part of God's plan to shift humanity back toward Him. None of them woke up knowing what would happen! I'm not trying to write or rewrite doctrine, but I do think it is imperative we adopt an attitude of giving Him the space to lead the way.

I do know that when the Spirit comes, there is a tangible shift. When we are willing to let Him do what He wants, He does nothing short of filling us up to overflowing with enabling, loving power that can work miracles. The timing and method isn't necessarily the same for everyone, but the end result of a changed life is remarkable to see.

In yesterday's passage, Jesus gave His disciples their first dose of this all-consuming perfect love, setting the stage for the disciples to be cured of fear. In this passage, I believe we see that work finished. The Holy Spirit has not stopped giving those who ask what is needed. As awesome as this historical Pentecost moment is with the wind, fire, and supernatural linguistic abilities, knowing what I have experienced, there could be another point to this passage.

The point could be about the arrival of endowment of God on His children. Not since the garden of Eden had humankind been this close to God. Not since the world was perfect—when we were created blameless and without sin—could we walk and talk with the Lord this intimately. Not even Abraham, Moses, or King David had this level of communion with the Lord. He became available to be on the inside and so filled them with Himself that they became able to live in and for the purpose He designed.

The Spirit still works like this in believers. He conforms us into the image of the Son. He overcomes our flesh and puts calls on our lives to act for His purposes—that level of work requires unnatural power. He desires all creation to be immersed in His Spirit. Ask Him for His presence today.

Prayer

Come, Holy Spirit. I ask for Your presence and Your power to come into and upon my life. Help me to surrender to the mighty force of Your will moving me into pleasant places of purpose and the empowerment to do it in Your strength. Show me how to trust Your perfect timing in everything. I eagerly await what You will do in my life today. In Jesus' name, amen.

Thought

Has the wait for the Holy Spirit been worth it for you?

Group Discussion

1. What do you feel is the symbolism the Lord is communicating in the Holy Spirit coming in as wind, noise, and fire?
2. Think of a situation where you had no choice but to wait on the Lord to act. What did you learn in that time?
3. How have you seen the Holy Spirit move in power?

DAY 19

Heaven Come

> And it will be in the last days, says God, that I will pour out My Spirit on all humanity; then your sons and your daughters will prophesy, your young men will see visions, and your old men will dream dreams. I will even pour out My Spirit on My male and female slaves in those days, and they will prophesy.
>
> —Acts 2:17–18

Recently, my family and I were on a trip with my husband's tribe from his hometown. One morning toward the end of the trip, I was up as the sun was rising. I had a lot on my mind because we were headed home, and my thoughts were becoming consumed with all we had to do when we got back.

I was praying, but I wasn't. I was praying without really forming words; but being a verbal processor, I reached a point where I felt an overwhelming urge to speak. Rather than allow words to pour out of my mouth, I stopped my natural tendency and asked the Lord a question: "What should I be praying for?"

I sat with my eyes closed for what felt like a long time. I started to become afraid I would miss what the Lord wanted to say, or I'd missed it already. As much as I like to talk, I'm also stubborn, so I decided to stay quiet and keep listening. After what felt like eternity, I opened my eyes and looked out on this beautiful scene of brilliant green and golden sunlight. The sun was pouring down on this cove of trees near where we'd parked our houseboat. I blinked a lot to allow my eyes to adjust. As I did, only one word pressed in my heart and mind: *heaven*.

When I look at this passage from Acts—which is the fulfillment of the prophecy from the prophet Joel in the Old Testament—heaven coming is what I see. God's will is being spoken and acted out on earth. As the Holy Spirit enters in and dwells in our hearts, that's exactly what we have: a total, unfettered reflection of heaven coming. The Holy Spirit immersing us, taking more of us into Himself is what "Thy kingdom come, Thy will be done" (Matt. 6:10) really looks like. It is absolute truth and divine presence in our dimension, in our very bodies, and overtaking our souls.

Thanks to Jesus' death and resurrection, what could never dwell together before now can. That reality shift in this passage also tells me all people have access to God—regardless of race, age, gender, or social status. It doesn't matter who or what you have been, you are invited to swim in the ocean of the loving presence of God Almighty.

Following that word on that brilliant morning, I walked through my relationships. My prayers were emboldened by imagining heaven coming into each circumstance. I thought of my husband, my children, and their future; my mom and my brother; my closest friends; and my church community. I lifted up a heart full of glorious hope, putting each person and situation right into God's hands. The light of that morning reminded me of the light shining into all the dark places. The heat I felt in that summer sunrise told me God's love would warm even the coldest spots in life. It is in, by, and through the Holy Spirit in us heaven will come to earth.

Prayer

Come, Holy Spirit. I place all that I am and all I have into Your hands and into Your light. I thank You for transforming it all for Your glory. Let heaven come! In Jesus' name, amen.

Thought

Take a few moments to listen to what the Spirit is speaking in this passage and the meaning it has for your life.

Group Discussion

1. Can you recount an experience where the Lord unexpectedly but powerfully spoke to you about how He was working in your life?
2. What do the words "heaven come" mean to you?
3. How can that transform your prayers for yourself, your loved ones, and your world?

DAY 20

The Glue That Holds Us Together

> This hope will not disappoint us, because God's love has been poured out in our hearts through the Holy Spirit who was given to us.
>
> —Romans 5:5

Our faith in Christ makes all things possible. Our trust and belief is what opens the door for this promise to be attained—the realized promise of the Holy Spirit poured into our hearts. The promise of His love poured into us was signed on the dotted line two thousand years ago. It's just been waiting for us to catch up. Like wet cement, God's love is waiting for us to step in it so it can solidify around our feet and hold us in His foundation.

The Holy Spirit is the giver of the truth. He is the very breath of God. He is the One who makes us come alive. He teaches us who we really are and how to live the way Jesus did. He shows us who God really is, and what He thinks of us. As we seek His wisdom and grace, His continual witness compels us. As a result, this love relationship matures. The love of God continues to do more. It conceives and bears hope—a hope that does not disappoint.

This hope born from the heart of God is able to pour in when we ask for the experience of the Holy Spirit. Hope changes us—it helps us to see beyond our circumstances and expectations. This hope gives us strength to endure tough times. It also grows when we cultivate and cherish it, as well as when we have doubts and lean into the Lord for His comfort. The more we connect with the Holy Spirit, the faster hope gains ground in our minds and souls. This hope the Holy Spirit abundantly gives is the guarantee of our safety and security. He makes that simple virtue of hope the superglue that holds us together in the hands of God.

Picture it this way: Have you ever gotten superglue on your hands? If you have, you know what I mean. It sticks like nothing else—except for the Spirit of God. He sticks closer than a brother. He sticks inside our ribs, inside our hearts. He bonds with us, and within His presence comes the love of God. It can never be removed or revoked.

As much as He is a person, He is also a gift of God. He is the grace and love of God personified. He has character and grants us purpose. We must change for that to become reality, but it is good change. His permanence is beyond our understanding. There will come a time when the sun won't rise, the calendar won't move, and everything will pass away.

Yet, this gift of God will never fail. The Holy Spirit is this gift—the pouring of His everlasting love into our hearts by putting the perfect representative in our hearts. He is the One who raises up unfailing hope from the birth of His coming. He will right us in an upside-down world. He will stick by and with us. He is the glue that holds our lives together and always will.

Prayer

Come, Holy Spirit. Put the glue of Your presence inside my heart, mind, and circumstances today. Create a hope that will never disappoint into my spirit so I may be one with You; and make all I think or say pleasing in Your sight. I welcome Your transforming power and look forward to the evidence of good change happening inside and around me. In Jesus' name, amen.

Thought

Is there a place in your heart or a circumstance in your life where you've lost your hope for God's transforming power?

Group Discussion

1. When you think of hope, what imagery comes to mind?
2. How has hope sustained you in difficult times?
3. Where can you give more opportunity to the Holy Spirit to pour into you?

DAY 21

The Life Meant for You

> Therefore, no condemnation now exists for those in Christ Jesus, because the Spirit's law of life in Christ Jesus has set you free from the law of sin and death.
>
> —Romans 8:1–2

Romans 8 is one of my favorite chapters in all of Scripture. It includes some of the deepest, most rich teaching on the life Jesus desires for us. One term you might hear for it is "the Spirit-filled life," or even "the abundant life in Christ." Methodist founder John Wesley called it "a life of holiness."

This new life begins with a new order, a new position in relation to God. It is technically a reorder or a do-over tracing back to Adam and Eve. Our access to

God is no longer determined by how many boxes we've checked on the spiritual to-do list or how well we obey. Now, under Christ, through the power of the Holy Spirit, we relate to God on how many boxes Jesus checked. He is the only one to ever check them all. It is a reversal of fortune in the most dramatic fashion. Sin wiped out all of our ability to check boxes, but Jesus came to do it for us. We get credit with Jesus' work! That is an amazing reality we live in now.

It is the most expensive gift we've ever received. It is a gift so costly we can never repay it or live up to the standard of being worthy, save without the help of God Himself. I imagine that fact must have been in the back of Paul's mind as he laid out what it is like to live according to the Spirit.

If we live always conscious of our sin and unworthiness, we will squander this gift and His grace. We will adopt a slave mentality where we have to work to please God. Good work is a part of our faith but a "work to be worthy" identity directly opposes Jesus' finished work. When we live from that place, we don't make the most of the Spirit giving to us.

However, when we live under what Paul calls "the Spirit of adoption" (Rom. 8:15), we learn to respond to our identity as firstborn heirs with the same rights and privileges as the firstborn over all creation. In that place, we have liberty to explore who the Lord created us to be. In that place, we find the power to overcome our past and what holds us back in the present. We live whole and grow in wholeness. That freedom is designed to create humble, Spirit-seeking children of God.

It's a choice we make every day, the choice of which heart and mind position to live from. It is a waste of time trying to gain what's already been given to us and miss the miraculous hand of the Spirit on our lives. Healing for the disease of fear and feeling unworthy can be found. What's more, it leads us to an exciting, hope-filled identity that carries the power of God's redemption with us wherever we go.

This passage confronts me with that choice. It's true, I will make mistakes, but I don't have to live bound by the fear of never being worthy again. I can spread my wings and fly as the Spirit lifts me up. I will run and not grow weary as the Spirit empowers me. I will walk and not fall over exhausted as the Spirit strengthens me. The Spirit's law is life, not fear, which leads to death. This is the life Jesus designed for us in His own life, death, and resurrection. Are you ready for it?

Prayer

Come, Holy Spirit. Reveal where I feel unworthy of Your gift of righteousness. Free me from the fear that I will never measure up so I don't desire what Jesus died to give me. Heal me and show me how to fly. In Jesus' name, amen.

Thought

If you have ever been trapped by fear, what would it be like to live free from it?

Group Discussion

1. What connotations do the phrases "Spirit-filled" or a "life of holiness" stir in your mind?
2. What healing and wholeness have you found in walking with Christ?
3. What would happen if the church focused on seeking the Spirit?

DAY 22

The New Normal

However, you are not [living] in the flesh [controlled by the sinful nature] but in the Spirit, if in fact the Spirit of God lives in you [directing and guiding you]. But if anyone does not have the Spirit of Christ, he does not belong to Him [and is not a child of God]. If Christ lives in you, though your [natural] body is dead because of sin, your spirit is alive because of righteousness [which He provides]. And if the Spirit of Him who raised Jesus from the dead lives in you, He who raised Christ Jesus from the dead will also give life to your mortal bodies through His Spirit, who lives in you.

—Romans 8:9–11 AMP

I'm glad we are still in Romans 8; I love this chapter so much. The changes in my heart have been won from the inside out. The most accelerated changes have come from the realization of the power of what Paul is saying in this chapter. Today's verse is a conditional promise—an "if, then" statement so often found in Scripture. Simply put: if the Spirit is in you (that same Spirit who formed the world and raised Jesus from the dead), everything else in you is brought back to life.

In writing to the Roman church, Paul shows us how to live with this very-present power. It is a new center. Our flesh is no longer on top. What the Spirit wants is what we should strive to get. Our flesh is strong though. Those long-held beliefs and behaviors that lead us to try and get what we want don't die easily. Thankfully, our futures have changed completely and irrevocably. Much of the fun of a Spirit-filled life is found in the process of that ongoing revelation.

When our middle daughter, Sophia, finished her treatment for cancer in July 2011 at age five, I wondered what the future held. It wasn't going to be about going to the hospital every week. There was now an adjustment to be made, as we figured out how to deal with life after the war against cancer. Our visits to the hospital and the panic attacks I developed early on in that process did not immediately go away once we were home. I feared I would have them for the rest of my life. They did taper off but would pop up unexpectedly. I was being forced to relearn who I was, and it was hell.

I know now those months were the beginning of something amazing, our new normal. Our lives had to find a new center after being turned upside down. And we did. We gained purpose and empathy. The Holy Spirit's presence enhanced that work in us. I look back now and see the hidden moments of joy in all that pain. I hoped for that in those months of treatment but couldn't picture it. Those months after her treatment continued to reveal how much God was (and still is) with us.

Life with the Holy Spirit is like emerging from a war. You have to put in the effort of knowing who He is and who you are with Him as the center of your life. He is the new normal, not your own thoughts and desires. It is a process to understand what He is doing in your life. We are no longer tied to death but to life. When Sophia was in treatment, her life was tied to doing all we could to make sure she survived. When it was over and she was healed, we had to learn how to make sure we did all we could to teach her how to thrive in this life.

If you have engaged with the Holy Spirit through this time, that's where you are—alive and no longer fighting for survival. You are learning how to thrive. The life Jesus came to give is there if the Spirit is in you. Your job today is to participate in the process and learn. Your job is to choose that new normal.

Prayer

Come, Holy Spirit, and teach me more about my new way of being in and with You. Show me life where I see death. Let me feel Your presence with me today. In Jesus' name, amen.

Thought

What do you see in you or another's life as needing the resurrection power of the Holy Spirit?

Group Discussion

1. Have you ever experienced a transition out of a crisis situation and had to learn how to live again?
2. How long did it take and what was involved?
3. How has that revealed the presence of God to you and what the Spirit is doing in your life?

DAY 23

Help for the Restless

In the same way the Spirit also joins to help us in our weakness, because we do not know what to pray for as we should, but the Spirit Himself intercedes for us with unspoken groanings.

—Romans 8:26

I love that we have an inside man. The Holy Spirit is someone who can take my jumbled thoughts and emotions to make them make sense. He goes beyond that to make them powerful prayers. He presents our prayers to God in such a way that leads the Father to act on our behalf. So many of the messes I've been in are self-inflicted. I'm so relieved I have the Holy Spirit to help me, a real and ever-present help.

Even in prayer, I often have my motives and intentions at heart. I want to get what I want, and it is hard to submit to the idea that God knows what is best for me and for others. I am constantly champing at the bit, constantly fighting to do God's will. That struggle causes unrest in my soul. It causes stress and sleepless nights. There is nothing good in it for us when we are constantly trying to get what we want or what God has revealed in our own power. If we try and make it happen before the timing is right through our own efforts and ability, we will hit a breaking point. We will become discouraged, doubtful, and even have a hard time rising up to believe in that good future He has planned.

The hardest thing to do sometimes is admit I am weak, I can't do it, and my way isn't working. The situation the Lord has me in could very well be less than ideal. There have even been times I've spent in the wilderness, in a season of hardship. Yet, these times are not the ultimate plan. These are times to learn to rest in Him—no matter what is happening around me. When we fall back into trust, we fall into the arms of the One meant to help us. The Holy Spirit wants us to unclench our hands and take His so we can pray in a way only possible by faith. He wants us to let Him carry the weight, the burden of our needs. If He has promised to do something for us, He will follow through on it. It will happen.

The Holy Spirit can and will teach us as we wait. He will empower us to keep going when the way is rocky and we stumble. He holds on firmly enough to keep us from hitting the ground, like a toddler walking with his or her parents. His yoke is supposed to be light and easy, so when it is not, that's a sure sign we are taking on too much of the load ourselves.

He asks us to come into His rest. The first step is to admit you are restless. That might require some wordless groanings as you turn away from your self-made source for rest. He will rush in to meet your needs with additional resources you've forgotten, like peace, clarity, and wisdom. He wants to fill us with love because we need His encompassing love to endure in this harsh, self-seeking world.

In admitting your needs, He will help you to see the blessing of pulling back. It is a great relief to find an oasis in the middle of the storm. There is nothing wrong with taking time to recharge, to find your own path to wholeness and healing. He will always show us the path back to a restful place when He will take our needs to the throne room of God. He takes our mess and makes it make sense. Crawl up in His lap today and find the help He so desires to give you.

Prayer

Come, Holy Spirit, so that I might let go of my restlessness to find my rest in You. I unclench my hands and take Yours. I fall into Your lap in order that You might help things make sense again. What a gift it is to be able to turn to You and know You are taking my needs to the Father! Thank you! Thank You for teaching me to depend on You. I trust you. In Jesus' name, amen.

Thought

Spend time in silence picturing yourself giving everything over to the Holy Spirit.

Group Discussion

1. Have you ever run out of words in prayer?
2. What do you find is the biggest benefit of running out of words in prayer?
3. What are the lessons you've learned during times of groanings, or in the wilderness?

DAY 24

Tangible Love

> Now may the God of hope fill you with all joy and peace as you believe in Him so that you may overflow with hope by the power of the Holy Spirit.
>
> —Romans 15:13

This is one of my life verses. I use it in my prayers for others a lot, especially with my children. It is so full of the reality of the person of the Holy Spirit. It demonstrates the mission and ministry of the Holy Spirit. He came to give us hope, joy, peace, and power—just like what we see in Jesus.

This verse also shows me the relationship between the Father and the Spirit. The Father is love and the Spirit is hope. Where there is no hope, love is lacking. There can be no peace with the Father where the Spirit does not abide. Conversely, where the Father has sent

His love, the Spirit encapsulates it with hope. We grow in these spiritual character traits of hope, joy, peace, and power the more we allow the Spirit to work in us. They are the evidence of connection—the fruit that will be produced when we are firmly planted in the soil of the Father's love.

Two years ago, I embraced this verse. I loved it so much that I had a bracelet inscribed with it. I wore that bracelet every day. It was my tangible reminder of the promise I felt God had spoken directly to me. However, I wore that treasure only a few short months before the Lord moved me to give it to my friend Audrey. On a Monday morning I felt the Lord saying she needed the reminder of this promise more than I did. He'd used the bracelet to write it on my heart and in my mind over a few months. Now, someone else needed to learn it. I didn't like this idea of God's. No, I did not like it at all.

Minutes after this unwanted message arrived in my heart, I went to a weekly prayer group Audrey and I attend together. The impulse to give her the bracelet was strong and growing. It was like Edgar Allen Poe's *The Tell-Tale Heart*. My flesh and my spirit were fighting a heavy battle, but I knew what I had to do. I explained to our group leader what was going on inside of me, and she went to get me a card to put it in. She handed me a box of cards, and the card on top of the stack had this verse—Romans 15:13—on the front! My jaw hit the floor. The direction the Lord was giving me couldn't have been more obvious. I hastily wrote Audrey a note, put my bracelet in it, and handed it over before I changed my mind.

I did mourn the loss of my bracelet, but I knew I loved my friend more. Over the next few months, that symbol of love sustained Audrey's faith during a very dark and desperate season. At the time, I didn't know the extent of her need, but the Holy Spirit did. He knew she needed that tangible reminder of His promise and that someone loved her. He knew she was hurting and doubting His love. Now knowing more fully what He did for her in that time, I would give her a thousand bracelets if I had to do it over again.

It was the Holy Spirit who carried her through. She is in a much better place now; her hope is full to overflowing and passing it along. Last year, Audrey passed the bracelet to another woman who needed that special tangible reminder of the love of the Father that overflows with hope by the power of the Holy Spirit.

Prayer

Come, Holy Spirit. Open my eyes to see the tangible reminders of Your all-powerful love in my life. Show me someone I can give that hope to today, through Your power. I welcome the opportunity. In Jesus' name, amen.

Thought

What kind of reminder of the Father's love is the Holy Spirit revealing to you right now?

Group Discussion

1. Share an experience with someone today about how the Holy Spirit has moved you to act in a way that opened up an opportunity for another to experience the Father's love and hope.
2. What tangible reminders of God's love and hope have you received from others?
3. Is there anyone in your life who is desperate for hope? Ask the Holy Spirit to use you to be a tangible reminder of His love for that person.

DAY 25

The Importance of Knowing God

> Now God has revealed these things to us by the Spirit, for the Spirit searches everything, even the depths of God. For who among men knows the thoughts of a man except the spirit of the man that is in him? In the same way, no one knows the thoughts of God except the Spirit of God. Now we have not received the spirit of the world, but the Spirit who comes from God, so that we may understand what has been freely given to us by God.
>
> —1 Corinthians 2:10–12

The reason we've been given Jesus' Spirit is to know Him and be one with Him and the Father. This is the most important thing to know and the biggest reason to cultivate a relationship with the Spirit. It is through Him we know Jesus better. And if we know Jesus, we know the Father.

A lack of knowledge breeds fear. When we are fearful, we get consumed with our own needs, our own gifts, and our own future. We grasp at straws and we forget the other. When we don't know God, we suspect He doesn't like us. We suspect He is bent on judging, not saving us. We fear Him, but not in the Old Testament way that means to honor and respect. Our hearts start seeing the evil of this world as His judgment. Rather than look for His goodness, we start to look over our shoulder. When things are going well, we begin to wonder when the other shoe will drop.

However, knowledge brings relationship. In relationship, we lose suspicion and start to think the best, not the worst, of people. It is the same with God and the Holy Spirit.

He has been given to us because His delight is to teach us deep things, revelations of the concerns at the heart of the Godhead. He is the Comforter because when we understand things, we are comforted. It is when things remain a mystery we start to get uncomfortable. We need His help to find peace and the wisdom required to understand the spiritual life Jesus showed was possible.

This process takes a long time. We don't live in a culture built or suited to that. We want it all instantly.

Yet this one skill, being dedicated to the pursuit of the knowledge of God, is something the Holy Spirit offers no other way of living can. It isn't just head knowledge, but heart fulfillment.

One of the biggest lessons I've learned from my husband is that the first one to speak loses. He is not the extrovert I am. I was trained in my sales career to have answers on the tip of my tongue. But as an engineer, he thinks deeply on things, and sometimes for a very long time. When he speaks, it is much more of a solution, versus the Band-Aids I usually try and slap onto people's problems.

There are deep truths that take a long time in coming. It can be better that way, so they come from deep down, rooted in truth, and not able to be shaken. What concerns God can be made known to us and it will be. If you have asked and the answer hasn't come yet, be wary of the devil's favorite trap of confusing silence with God ignoring you. Believe He is preparing you and your circumstances for the answer. The Spirit wants to meet you where that deep in you calls out of His deep, and from there the promise will bubble up.

Prayer

Come, Holy Spirit. Sustain me with Your presence and help me trust Your character and wisdom will comfort me as I wait and seek Your face. Help me to see the treasure of who You are. In Jesus' name, amen.

Thought

Have you ever fallen in the trap of thinking God is ignoring you?

Group Discussion

1. What is the best counsel you can give someone about the way the Holy Spirit works?
2. Is there a situation where you can apply your own advice to your life or a situation?
3. Why is it better to wait than to rush ahead of God?

DAY 26

The Jesus Glow

> Now the Lord is the Spirit, and where the Spirit of the Lord is, there is freedom. We all, with unveiled faces, are looking as in a mirror at the glory of the Lord and are being transformed into the same image from glory to glory; this is from the Lord who is the Spirit.
>
> —2 Corinthians 3:17–18

What we've received from God lasts; and what we gain in Christ is glorious. Indeed, what we've received can't be covered. The lights the Holy Spirit ignites in us cannot be hidden under a bushel or anywhere else (as I often sing with my youngest).

Our lights of faith in God keep us connected to Him. Jesus coming out of the tomb reveals our ultimate hope, the unchangeable fact of eternity on earth. We claim that victory without shame—that is our "Jesus Glow." It is the face the Lord wants us to turn to the world to light it up, as evidence and proof His mercy is available to all mankind.

I have a friend who says when strangers ask if they know you, it's the Jesus Glow they are recognizing. She says they are recognizing the very life-giving presence of God within us. We were all created to have it; and when the switch is flipped at salvation, we can see it in someone else. Like with John the Baptist in his mother's womb, our spirits connect in a leap of recognition.

I've seen the Jesus Glow come on someone in a very dramatic fashion. When she released twenty-eight years of pain, abuse, and bitterness, the newfound freedom literally took wrinkles and lines off her face. After she received the Holy Spirit's fullness, she looked like she'd had the most effective face-lift ever. She finally was full, her empty places met by the grace and love of God. Her soul found the life it always craved and the Spirit had been given to her in abundance.

My friend's Jesus Glow hasn't faded, although that experience was several years ago. Her life circumstances weren't magically altered; in fact, they got worse after that experience with the Holy Spirit. But we both believe this radical encounter with the Holy Spirit happened when it did so that she could endure with hope, and ultimately be an instrument that brings others to the freedom in Christ she's found. It is a freedom born of forgiveness and trust. It is a freedom only found through believing God loves her enough to give her Himself.

It is the Spirit of the Lord who wants to lift those burdens and bring rest to us. It's the kind of rest we can't get from a mattress, a pill, or anywhere else. It may not come as dramatically as it did for my friend. My own glow has come over time. It has been a daily submission, holding my hands out to God to give Him what I have, and accepting His fullness in return.

When we ask, the Lord will show up. He always does. He sweeps in with a fire that warms us up from the cold shadows of this life. As we sit in His presence, He fans our own flames and makes our cheeks pink too.

Prayer

Come, Holy Spirit. Come and warm any cold places in my heart. Show me what it feels like to burn with You and for Your glory. Let the glow of the Spirit be on my face today. In Jesus' name, amen.

Thought

Write down a few thoughts on what you feel freedom in the Holy Spirit looks like. Then ask the Holy Spirit to make that freedom more abundant in your life.

Group Discussion

1. Have you ever known someone who had that Jesus Glow?
2. What was their story?
3. What kind of impact did it have on your own walk of faith?

DAY 27

God of Renewal

When you heard the message of truth, the gospel of your salvation, and when you believed in Him, you were also sealed with the promised Holy Spirit. He is the down payment of our inheritance, for the redemption of the possession, to the praise of His glory.

—Ephesians 1:13–14

Our faith comes down to this simple fact: through Jesus, we are saved by grace. Because Jesus is ultimately concerned with the healing and redemption of His creation, He wasn't willing to leave us alone. He promised to never leave or forsake us. A replacement had to be sent. Jesus had a limited time on earth, but He wasn't content to leave us. Jesus was the promised Immanuel, or "God with us," until His work was done.

When He went home, He sent us the ultimate prize, "God in us."

Still, this third person isn't a Jesus cardboard cutout—he is a different person, although a very close kin. The Holy Spirit is the power of God, the force of His love—that is greater than having Jesus walk beside us. Because of who the Holy Spirit is and where He lives—in our spirits—we get the same power, wisdom, and ability to sacrificially love all the time, not just when Jesus is physically around. We get a better deal with the Holy Spirit. He is the evidence of renewal, trading all that we are for all that God has to offer. It's a priceless deal! We could never have made this deal, so Jesus made it for us.

We have nothing to give back—nothing to offer as a down payment. So, He signs, closes, and seals the deal. He gives it all. We are never on the losing side again. While we were born to perish, He gives us abundant life, now and forever. It's for a specific purpose, for the renewal of all of creation. He is all about renewal, which we see each spring. His design is a visible reality in nature.

He wants to use us to be the vessels of renewal too. We have destinies to fulfill, as ministers of reconciliation. The Father's plan is now complete by the work of the Son through the presence of the Holy Spirit in us. Yet, He didn't stop there—He gives us more and more and more.

We can make a different choice, though. We don't have to accept the more He wants to give. We can settle for less. We can talk ourselves out of what the Lord seeks to give. Maybe you have reached that point, or God seems to be done giving. Maybe you feel saved of your sins but that's it. There is more waiting. Jesus revealed there was always more in the mind of the Father, and He often said so. Settling was never in Jesus' nature.

It comes back to us and our choices. Here is the question we must answer: If God pulled out all the stops to save us, why would we think He would ever stop bringing us further into this new life of grace?

God is not content to save a little—He must save to the utmost. He desires not only to save the soul, but the heart, mind, and body. Complete wholeness is what He longs to give us. It is the kind of life He lived, fully integrated in the heart of the Father. We get the best God has to offer because we get Him living with and in us.

Prayer

Come, Holy Spirit, and renew me—mind, body, and soul. I ask that the truth of the promise of Your coming wash over me and give me the wholeness You desire for me. Fill me with a holy desire to praise You and bring You glory. Show me the reality of this inheritance in my life and make me a vessel to reveal the renewal happening in others. In Jesus' name, amen.

Thought

Take a moment and ask the Holy Spirit what situation or relationship He wants to renew for you.

Group Discussion

1. How does the promised inheritance of the Holy Spirit lead us to renewal?
2. What stories of redemption have made the most impact on you?
3. Can knowing you are sealed for redemption change how you approach a relationship or difficult circumstances?

DAY 28

Call Me "Papa"

And because you are sons, God has sent the Spirit of His Son into our hearts, crying, "*Abba*, Father!"

—Galatians 4:6

Sonship is a relationship other children don't have. In Roman and Hebrew culture, only sons—firstborns, in particular—received certain rights. All of humanity is part of God's family, but because we've embraced His firstborn Son, Jesus, we are elevated to the same status not only as firstborn heirs, but adopted firstborns. We are positioned right next to the Father with Christ, with the same privileges, authority, and responsibility.

Because God views us as sons, we have unprecedented access to the Father's heart. We are first in line. He hears us, watches over us, and provides all we need. Just as I come running up the stairs when one of my girls calls to me in the middle of the night, so the Lord comes running to us when we call.

The Holy Spirit in us makes this possible. Without Him, we couldn't cry out with the same connection. We couldn't call God *Abba*, the word for "daddy" in Aramaic. It is a moldable word. It speaks of the kind of comfort, security, and identity only a father gives. This Abba kind of father meets our all needs, gives us purpose, and keeps us safe. Like a security blanket, this father is the kind of warmth that wraps around us and holds us close.

I never felt like I could call God "Daddy," although that's how this word is often translated. After my dad died suddenly in September 2015, I realized I'd always struggled to call God "Father." I had a good dad—really, the best. The picture that comes to my mind when I visualize the word "dad" is him. With his passing, the trouble in relating to God this way started to surface. I discovered there were ideas in my heart that had to be cleaned out in order for me to really embrace God as Father. I didn't have a father anymore. I needed Him to step into that place in a big way.

During a prayer session, I was shocked when the Lord spoke to me, "I'm not your dad. I don't want you to call Me dad. You had a dad and I'm not him. I'm not your daddy either. I want you to call Me something different. I want you to call Me your Papa."

In that moment, I felt the Lord was honoring my dad's place in my life, but was calling me to go deeper with Him. The Holy Spirit gave me a safe word to connect with Him better than I ever have. It's taken me some months to process that revelation, along with my grief; and I'm still learning to live in it. But I do know my time with God is easier and richer than ever. Even as I miss my dad, I feel the peace that comes from the presence of my Papa—the Holy Spirit—as He helps me look back, look around, and look forward.

Prayer

Come, Holy Spirit, and where there is loss, shower me with Your comfort. Thank You for the unprecedented access and privilege of being in Your presence right now. Help me to know how to call You my *Abba*. I want to feel connected to my heavenly Father through a nurturing relationship with You. In Jesus' name, amen.

Thought

Does anything hinder you from relating to God as Father? If so, take a few minutes to let the Holy Spirit speak comfort, healing, and peace into you.

Group Discussion

1. What it does it mean to you to have the Spirit of the Son working in your life?
2. Do you think the church operates from the mind-set of a son or an orphan?
3. What would happen if the church shook off any orphan-mind-set-driven operations and lived in our privileges in Christ?

DAY 29

True Craftsmanship Underneath

> He saved us—not by works of righteousness that we had done, but according to His mercy, through the washing of regeneration and renewal by the Holy Spirit. He poured out this Spirit on us abundantly through Jesus Christ our Savior, so that having been justified by His grace, we may become heirs with the hope of eternal life.
>
> —Titus 3:5–7

When I worked in the corporate world, I had a few nicknames. "Tiger Lady" and "Xena Warrior Princess" were two favorites of my team members. They were appropriate because I was intense, driven, and competitive. I am of the generation that taught girls can do anything boys can do. In the environment I was in, I had a lot to prove, and that attitude served me well. I was successful mostly because I pushed myself to be better than my peers—to win and not look back. My performance defined my value, which made for a difficult transition to make as a stay-at-home mom!

I was still working my sales job when I came back to the Lord at age twenty-nine. I started to realize there'd been a tangible shift. That drive to win, to have my worth defined by how successful I was in the eyes of others, wasn't gone. Yet the talons of that dangerous works-based spirit weren't dug as deep in my heart. Don't get me wrong, play a game with me and you'll find I am still just as competitive. Still, that competitiveness drove my self-worth. My identity as "the Tiger Lady" was being stripped away, slowly and surely, like a dull varnish. God wanted to reveal the true craftsmanship underneath.

I've watched my mom restore furniture. It is a long, laborious process. It's a good analogy for what happened and continues to happen in my soul through the work of the Holy Spirit. He is poured out on us, coating us with grace, mercy, and hope. He is the stain remover, taking off the layers of identity He did not give us. He corrects our vision and removes those dangerous parasites and weeds caused by this fallen existence. Sometimes, multiple layers come off. In others, it is little by little, but He stays in there. He works until the work is complete and the true crafted masterpiece is revealed.

I know I'm different than who I was more than a decade ago. I have learned (the hard way) my old, bossy, and scrambling ways don't work. I can't flex my own muscles to bring about His kingdom purposes. It is through a process of responding to the invitations God gives to work and partner alongside His Spirit. But first, we must hold out our hands so He can scrub away the stickiness of our fleshly selves to reveal the true, gleaming real wood underneath, originally created for very good works.

I've traded "the Tiger Lady" for trying to be a lamb He carries, guides, comforts, teaches, corrects, and cares for all day, every day. The Holy Spirit reminds me regularly who is really doing the work of transformation in my life. Anything significant I've done has been because He has done it in and through me. I am only a willing participant and conduit of His love and power to others.

My intensity now comes from my changed desires and motivations. I want to love well, to live better than I did yesterday, as I more fully become the beloved. I know I don't have to prove anything, but it's still a journey to live from that place. There's no longer a need to compete and work for God because as I rest in the hands of my

Maker, I will share in the goodness He is revealing. It's a beautiful partnership where He does all the work.

Prayer

Come, Holy Spirit, and show me how to be justified—to find my worth in You and nothing else. Show me what it means to live as an heir, where the resources are abundant and require no competition. Allow me to follow—to let You do the work and find my rest as Your beloved. In Jesus' name, amen.

Thought

What have you experienced as you've begun the process of letting the Holy Spirit strip you of your old identity and give you new life and purpose in Him?

Group Discussion

1. What do you think is the danger of working for righteousness instead of resting in it?
2. How is the Holy Spirit regenerating your life and refreshing your heart?
3. What do you think Paul means when he writes we are "heirs with the hope of eternal life"?

DAY 30

Conscious of Grace

Then he sat down right beside God and waited for his enemies to cave in. It was a perfect sacrifice by a perfect person to perfect some very imperfect people. . . . The Holy Spirit confirms this:

This new plan I'm making with Israel isn't going to be written on paper, isn't going to be chiseled in stone; This time "I'm writing out the plan *in* them, carving it on the living tissue of their hearts."

He concludes, I'll forever wipe the slate clean of their sins.

Once sins are taken care of for good, there's no longer any need to offer sacrifices for them.

—Hebrews 10:12, 15–18 (MSG)

There are days when all I can think about is my state of imperfection. I can't get away from what I've done wrong, thought wrong, or how I've just been wrong. And usually I take others, generally those who live with me, down that dark path with me. On those days, I get reminders of the constant scriptural theme of life in Christ: but God.

This verse points me to the reality that the Trinity has worked too hard to let us wallow in our own failing. We aren't meant to think primarily of ourselves, but to love Him first. It is this awareness that it isn't about me that He is constantly bringing to the forefront of my mind. He speaks in a variety of ways. He confirms His presence. He demonstrates, again and again, how He doesn't miss a thing. His point is never to condemn, only to bring me back to the reality that His perfection has forever trumped my imperfection.

We need those refreshers and reminders, which He provides gently but effectively. He has no desire to break us violently. He doesn't need to do that because He isn't about control. He wants to make Christ and the Father's heart known to us. That's how He changes desires and feelings. He wants the truth of His loving, faithful, merciful, and all-powerful nature to be a part of each heartbeat. The mystery of our faith is the Holy Spirit coming in so close as to bond with our very cells, in order that the external and eternal reality of God's sovereign, caring rule would become a part of our internal reality.

We still sin. That's also part of our reality. Until Jesus comes back, we will live in that tension. Still, there will be a day when the taint of our ancestral disobedience is removed forever. It is promised, and in the supernatural realm, it is finished. We just have to catch up to it. For those still living in the tension, though, we can take heart because sin no longer defines us—imperfection does, but who my perfect God is and what He has done has become my defining identity trait.

Through the power of the cross and resurrection, living in us through the Spirit, you get a do-over right this very second. You get to change your allegiance to anything not connected to His life-giving presence. Let the truth of His presence work itself out and pay attention. It is as if He is saying, "I'm teaching you to be aware, not of your sin, but of my grace. Tune into my perfection, not your imperfection."

Just as Jesus modeled, we have to pay more attention to the work of the Holy Spirit than to ourselves. Our part is to remember He is perfection in us. This is doing life with the Triune God. It is letting the Third Person advocate for us on earth, just as it is in heaven. It is total surrender that leads to total transformation, as long as we are open to the adventure of change. It will come and we will be all the better for it.

Prayer

Come, Holy Spirit, and make me aware of You and what You have already done in my spirit, soul, and body. As we continue this journey, let me feel and experience the grace by which You saved me, and make me open to each new adventure we will have together. Thank You for forever wiping my slate clean; I pray for the courage to continually be open to the truth You want to write on my heart instead. In Jesus' name, amen.

Thought

What adventure do you see the Lord setting up for the two of you to take together?

Group Discussion

1. Can you articulate the enemies the Lord has conquered for you? Who can you share that victory with today?
2. What truth about Himself has He freshly written on your heart through getting to know the Holy Spirit better?
3. If there is any doubt or struggle you have, ask Him to speak into that.

Appendix A
Attributes of the Holy Spirit

Creator

Day 1: Genesis 1:2
Day 2: Job 33:4
Day 3: Psalm 104:30
Day 10: Luke 1:35

Counselor

Day 5: Isaiah 11:2
Day 6: Ezekiel 36:25–27
Day 8: Matthew 3:11
Day 11: Luke 2:25
Day 12: John 3:8
Day 14: John 14:15–17
Day 15: John 14:26

Helper

Day 4: Nehemiah 9:20
Day 8: Matthew 3:11
Day 16: John 16:8–10

Day 23: Romans 8:26
Day 25: 1 Corinthians 2:10–12

Encourager

Day 7: Zechariah 4:6–7
Day 12: John 3:8
Day 16: John 16:8–10
Day 17: John 20:21–23
Day 20: Romans 5:5
Day 21: Romans 8:1–2
Day 22: Romans 8:9–11

Advocate

Day 9: Matthew 10:19–20
Day 18: Acts 2:2–4
Day 29: Titus 3:5–7
Day 30: Hebrews 10:12, 15–18

Comforter

Day 13: John 7:37–39
Day 16: John 16:8–10
Day 19: Acts 2:17–18
Day 24: Romans 15:13
Day 26: 2 Corinthians 3:17–18
Day 27: Ephesians 1:13–14
Day 28: Galatians 4:6
Day 29: Titus 3:5–7

Appendix B
Study Guide

Week 1—The Person of the Holy Spirit
Week 2—The Experience of the Holy Spirit
Week 3—The Work of the Holy Spirit
Week 4—The Gifts of the Holy Spirit
Week 5—The Implication of a Relationship with the Holy Spirit

Printed in the USA
CPSIA information can be obtained
at www.ICGtesting.com
LVHW010943230624
783773LV00006B/14

9 781628 245424